Guide To Adult

ADHD

:

Strategies For Managing Inattention In Daily Life

<u>Introduction</u>

let me quickly giddy you with these 10 Proverbs on ADHD

1. "A journey of a thousand miles begins with a single focus."

2. "A scattered mind gathers no peace."

3. "In the kingdom of attention, the focus is on the kings."

4. "A wandering mind finds no treasure."

5. "The key to success lies in unlocking your focus."

6. "A mind in chaos breeds confusion; a mind in order breeds clarity."

7. "In the land of concentration, the diligent are crowned."

8. "A scattered attention scatters opportunities."

9. "The focused mind is a powerful force."

10. "A steady hand steers the ship of attention through stormy seas."

Living with ADHD as an adult presents unique challenges that can impact every aspect of daily life. From struggles with attention and focus to difficulties with organization and time management, navigating the complexities of adult ADHD requires patience, understanding, and effective strategies. This book, "Guide to Adult ADHD: Strategies for Managing Inattention in Daily Life," is a comprehensive resource designed to provide practical guidance and support for adults living with ADHD. Whether you've recently been diagnosed or have been managing ADHD for years, this book offers valuable insights, tools, and techniques to help you thrive in your personal and professional life.

In the pages that follow, you'll discover a wealth of information about ADHD and its impact on adult functioning. We'll explore the unique manifestations of inattention in daily life and how they can affect everything from work performance and relationships to self-esteem and overall well-being. By gaining a deeper understanding of the challenges associated with ADHD, you'll be better equipped to develop strategies for managing symptoms and optimizing your quality of life.

Throughout this book, you'll find practical strategies and evidence-based approaches for managing inattention in various settings and contexts. From tips for improving focus and concentration to techniques for enhancing organization and time management, each chapter is designed to provide actionable guidance that you can implement in your daily life. Whether you're seeking support in the workplace, at home, or in social situations, you'll find strategies tailored to your unique needs and challenges.

In addition to practical strategies, this book also emphasizes the importance of self-awareness, self-compassion, and resilience in navigating the ups and downs of life with ADHD. By cultivating a positive mindset and embracing your strengths and limitations, you can build the confidence and resilience needed to overcome obstacles and achieve your goals. Throughout these pages, you'll find encouragement, inspiration, and validation as you embark on your journey towards greater self-understanding and empowerment.

It's important to recognize that managing ADHD is not a one-size-fits-all endeavor. What works for one person may not work for another, and it's okay to explore different approaches and strategies to find what works best for you. This book serves as a roadmap for navigating the complexities of adult ADHD, offering insights, tools, and resources to support you along the way. Whether you're seeking practical advice, validation, or a sense of community, you'll find support and guidance within these pages as you embark on your journey towards greater self-awareness and well-being.

Above all, remember that you are not alone in your journey with ADHD. Countless adults around the world face similar challenges and triumphs each day, and by sharing our experiences and insights, we can support one another on the path towards greater understanding, acceptance, and fulfillment. As you dive into the pages of this book, may you find inspiration, empowerment, and hope for the future as you navigate the complexities of adult ADHD and discover your own unique path to success and fulfillment.

Table Of Contents

Chapter 1: Understanding Inattention in Adult ADHD

- **Defining inattention: Symptoms, characteristics, and challenges**
- **Exploring the impact of inattention on daily life and functioning**
- **Recognizing the different manifestations of inattention in adult ADHD**

Defining inattention: Symptoms, characteristics, and challenges

Defining inattention in adults involves understanding its symptoms, characteristics, and the challenges it presents, particularly in the context of adult life and responsibilities. Here's a breakdown:

Symptoms of Inattention in Adults:

- Difficulty sustaining attention during tasks that require mental effort, such as work assignments, reading, or conversations.

- Frequently making errors or overlooking details due to lapses in concentration.

- Struggling to organize tasks and activities, leading to inefficiency and forgetfulness.

- Often losing or misplacing items needed for daily activities.

- Easily distracted by external stimuli or internal thoughts, resulting in difficulty staying focused on the task at hand.

- Difficulty following through on instructions or completing tasks, especially those that are mundane or repetitive.

Characteristics:

- Inattention in adults may manifest differently from how it does in children, often presenting as disorganization, forgetfulness, and difficulty with time management.

- It can occur independently or coexist with other symptoms of ADHD, such as impulsivity or hyperactivity.

- In adults, inattention may interfere with various aspects of life, including work, relationships, and personal responsibilities.

- It may contribute to feelings of frustration, low self-esteem, and impaired self-confidence, especially when individuals struggle to meet their own expectations or those of others.

Challenges:

- Inattention in adults can impact academic or professional performance, leading to difficulties meeting deadlines, maintaining productivity, and advancing in careers.

- It can strain interpersonal relationships, as individuals may appear forgetful, disorganized, or inattentive in social settings.

- Inattention may contribute to stress, anxiety, and feelings of inadequacy, particularly when individuals perceive themselves as falling short in their responsibilities or goals.

- Managing inattention requires developing coping strategies, establishing routines, and seeking support from professionals, peers, or support groups.

Understanding the symptoms, characteristics, and challenges of inattention in adults is essential for accurate diagnosis, effective treatment, and the development of strategies to help individuals manage their symptoms and improve their quality of life.

Exploring the impact of inattention on daily life and functioning

The impact of inattention on daily life and functioning can be profound and multifaceted, affecting various aspects of an individual's personal and professional life. Here's an exploration of its impact:

Work and Academic Performance:

- Inattention can hinder productivity and efficiency at work or school. Individuals may struggle to concentrate on tasks, leading to incomplete assignments, missed deadlines, and reduced performance.

- Difficulty staying focused during meetings, lectures, or studying sessions can impede learning and comprehension.

- Inattention may contribute to a pattern of underachievement or academic struggles, affecting grades, job opportunities, and career advancement.

Time Management and Organization:

- Inattention often correlates with poor time management skills and disorganization. Individuals may have difficulty prioritizing tasks, planning schedules, and adhering to deadlines.

- Procrastination is common among those with inattention, leading to last-minute rushes, increased stress, and subpar outcomes.

- Disorganization in personal and professional environments can exacerbate feelings of overwhelm and make it challenging to maintain order and efficiency.

Interpersonal Relationships:

- Inattention can strain relationships with family members, friends, and colleagues. Forgetfulness, inconsistency, and difficulty following through on commitments may erode trust and reliability.

- Communication may suffer as individuals with inattention may struggle to listen attentively, remember details from conversations, or stay engaged in interactions.

- Partners and family members may feel frustrated or neglected, especially if they perceive inattention as a lack of interest or consideration.

Emotional Well-being:

- The impact of inattention extends to emotional well-being, contributing to feelings of frustration, inadequacy, and low self-esteem.

- Individuals may experience heightened levels of stress, anxiety, or depression as they grapple with the challenges of managing their symptoms and navigating daily responsibilities.

- Coping mechanisms, such as avoidance or denial, may exacerbate emotional distress and perpetuate a cycle of dysfunction.

Safety and Health:

- Inattention can compromise safety, particularly in situations requiring vigilance or attention to detail, such as driving or operating machinery.

- Poor impulse control and risk assessment may increase the likelihood of accidents, injuries, or risky behaviors.

- Neglecting self-care routines, such as medication adherence or healthy lifestyle habits, may further compromise physical and mental well-being.

Understanding the impact of inattention on daily life and functioning underscores the importance of early recognition, accurate diagnosis, and comprehensive management strategies tailored to individual needs. By addressing underlying challenges and developing coping mechanisms, individuals can mitigate the negative effects of inattention and improve their overall quality of life.

Recognizing the different manifestations of inattention in adult ADHD

Recognizing the different manifestations of inattention in adult ADHD is crucial for understanding how the condition may present itself in various aspects of daily life. Here are some common manifestations:

Difficulty Sustaining Attention: Adults with ADHD often struggle to sustain attention, especially during tasks or activities that are repetitive, monotonous, or uninteresting. They may find themselves easily distracted or prone to zoning out, even during important conversations or activities.

Poor Time Management: Inattention can lead to difficulties in managing time effectively. Adults with ADHD may underestimate the time required to complete tasks, leading to chronic lateness, missed deadlines, and procrastination.

Forgetfulness: Forgetfulness is a common manifestation of inattention in adult ADHD. Individuals may forget appointments, deadlines, or important details in conversations. They may also struggle to remember where they put belongings or what they were supposed to do next.

Disorganization: Inattention can contribute to difficulties with organization and planning. Adults with ADHD may struggle to maintain tidy living or workspaces, frequently misplace items, and have trouble following through with tasks or projects due to disorganization.

Difficulty Following Instructions: Adults with ADHD may have difficulty following through with instructions or completing tasks that require sustained focus and attention to detail. They may become easily overwhelmed or confused by complex instructions, leading to errors or incomplete work.

Impulsivity: While impulsivity is often associated with hyperactivity, it can also manifest as impulsive decision-making or actions due to inattention in adult ADHD. Individuals may act on sudden urges or impulses without fully considering the consequences.

Inconsistent Performance: Adults with ADHD may experience fluctuations in performance and productivity, with periods of hyperfocus followed by periods of inattention or disengagement. They may excel in tasks that are highly stimulating or engaging but struggle with tasks that require sustained attention or follow-through.

Difficulty Listening: Inattention can manifest as difficulty listening attentively during conversations, meetings, or lectures. Adults with ADHD may struggle to maintain focus on the speaker's words, leading to misunderstandings or missed information.

Daydreaming or Mind Wandering: Inattention can also manifest as frequent daydreaming or mind wandering, where individuals become lost in their thoughts and lose track of the present moment. They may struggle to stay engaged in conversations or activities that require sustained attention.

Recognizing these different manifestations of inattention in adult ADHD can help individuals and their loved ones understand the challenges they may face and seek appropriate support and strategies for managing symptoms effectively. It's important to remember that ADHD symptoms can vary widely among individuals and may change over time, so personalized approaches to treatment and management are key.

Chapter 2: Developing Self-Awareness and Acceptance

- **Recognizing personal patterns of inattention**
- **Understanding the role of self-awareness in managing ADHD symptoms**
- **Cultivating self-compassion and acceptance in the face of inattention challenges**

Recognizing personal patterns of inattention

Recognizing personal patterns of inattention in adults is a crucial step toward understanding and managing Attention-Deficit/Hyperactivity Disorder (ADHD) or similar challenges. Here are some strategies to help recognize these patterns:

Self-Reflection and Observation: Take time to reflect on your daily routines, tasks, and interactions. Notice moments when your attention drifts, when you struggle to maintain focus, or when you feel overwhelmed by distractions.

Keep a journal or use a note-taking app to record instances of inattention throughout the day. Note the circumstances, triggers, and consequences of each episode.

Identifying Triggers and Environments: Identify specific situations, environments, or tasks that tend to exacerbate inattention. These may include noisy or cluttered spaces, tedious or repetitive tasks, or situations requiring sustained mental effort.

Pay attention to your emotional state and energy levels in different contexts. Notice whether certain moods, stressors, or fatigue contribute to inattention.

Recognizing Cognitive Patterns: Notice patterns of thought that accompany episodes of inattention. Are you easily distracted by external stimuli or internal thoughts? Do you have difficulty filtering out irrelevant information or staying on task?

Pay attention to your ability to maintain focus and sustain attention over time. Notice whether your attention tends to wander, and if so, what prompts these shifts.

Impact on Daily Functioning: Consider how inattention affects various aspects of your daily life and functioning, including work, relationships, and personal responsibilities. Notice patterns of forgetfulness, disorganization, or difficulty following through on tasks.

Reflect on feedback from others, such as colleagues, friends, or family members, regarding your attentional patterns and their impact on interactions and relationships.

Seeking Professional Input: Consider seeking input from mental health professionals, such as psychologists or psychiatrists, who specialize in adult ADHD assessment and treatment. They can provide diagnostic evaluation, insight into your attentional patterns, and recommendations for management strategies.

Participate in structured assessments or screenings designed to evaluate symptoms of ADHD and related challenges. These tools can help identify patterns of inattention and guide treatment planning.

By recognizing personal patterns of inattention, individuals can gain insight into their cognitive functioning, identify areas for improvement, and develop targeted strategies to manage symptoms effectively. Awareness and self-reflection are essential steps toward building resilience, optimizing functioning, and improving overall quality of life for adults with ADHD or similar attentional challenges.

Understanding the role of self-awareness in managing ADHD symptoms

Self-awareness plays a crucial role in managing ADHD symptoms in adults. Here's how:

Recognizing Symptoms: Self-awareness enables individuals to recognize and acknowledge the symptoms of ADHD they experience. This includes inattention, impulsivity, hyperactivity, and related challenges such as disorganization and forgetfulness.

Understanding Triggers: With self-awareness, individuals can identify specific triggers or situations that exacerbate their ADHD symptoms. They learn to recognize environments, tasks, or stressors that may lead to distraction, impulsivity, or difficulty focusing.

Monitoring Behavior and Reactions: Self-awareness involves monitoring one's own behavior, thoughts, and emotional reactions in real-time. Adults with ADHD can learn to observe how their symptoms manifest in various situations and how they respond to different stimuli.

Developing Coping Strategies: Self-awareness enables individuals to identify effective coping strategies for managing ADHD symptoms. By understanding their strengths and weaknesses, they can tailor strategies that work best for them, whether it's using organizational tools, implementing time management techniques, or practicing mindfulness and stress reduction exercises.

Taking Responsibility: Self-awareness fosters a sense of responsibility for managing ADHD symptoms and their impact on daily life. Individuals learn to take ownership of their challenges and actively seek strategies, support, and resources to address them.

Improving Communication: Being self-aware allows individuals to effectively communicate their needs, challenges, and preferences to others, such as family members, friends, or colleagues. It helps in explaining how ADHD symptoms may affect behavior, interactions, and relationships, fostering understanding and support from others.

Seeking Treatment and Support: Self-awareness often leads individuals to seek professional evaluation and treatment for ADHD. By recognizing the impact of symptoms on their functioning and well-being, they are more likely to reach out to mental health professionals for diagnosis, therapy, medication management, and other interventions.

Promoting Self-Advocacy: Self-awareness empowers individuals to advocate for themselves in various settings, including education, employment, and social environments. They can assert their needs, accommodations, and preferences to ensure they receive the support and accommodations necessary to thrive with ADHD.

In summary, self-awareness is a foundational aspect of managing ADHD symptoms in adults. It facilitates recognition, understanding, and proactive management of symptoms, leading to improved functioning, well-being, and quality of life.

<u>Cultivating self-compassion and acceptance in the face of inattention challenges</u>

Those with ADHD symptoms must learn to accept and be compassionate with themselves when they struggle with inattention. How to do it is as follows:

Acknowledge Your Flaws: Admit that having trouble focusing is a normal side effect of having ADHD. Recognize that everyone has shortcomings in addition to talents. Nobody is flawless.

Practice mindfulness: Mindfulness is being aware of your thoughts, emotions, and experiences in the present moment while avoiding judgment. You may witness your inattentional difficulties without passing judgment on them or yourself if you practice mindfulness.

Face Negative Self-Talk: Take note of and confront any negative self-talk that is connected to difficulties with inattention. Say something kind and understanding in lieu of self-critical ideas. Remember that having attention issues has nothing to do with your value as a person.

Honor Little Victories: Honor your accomplishments, no matter how little they may seem. Acknowledge the work you do to control your symptoms and the steps you've taken to become well.

Establish Reasonable Expectations: Taking into account your own advantages and disadvantages, establish reasonable expectations for yourself. Instead of comparing yourself to other people, concentrate on developing yourself.

Exercise self-compassion : By treating yourself with the same consideration and compassion that you would show a friend going through a comparable situation. Accept self-compassion as a potent instrument for promoting wellbeing and resilience.

Accept Imperfection: Acknowledge that you are flawed and that it's OK to make errors or run across obstacles. As you go through the highs and lows of managing your ADHD symptoms, give yourself space for improvement and education.

Seek Support: Be in the company of empathetic and understanding people who can provide you with consolation, compassion, and useful advice. Tell your family, close friends, or support groups about your experiences.

Concentrate on Your Strengths: Even in the face of difficulties, acknowledge and appreciate your special abilities. Stress your areas of strength and experience, and use them to your advantage to get over challenges and accomplish your objectives.

Take Care of Yourself: Give self-care tasks that advance your mental, emotional, and physical health first priority. Take part in enjoyable, stress-relieving, and fulfilling activities; they might include hobbies, physical activity, and quality time with loved ones.

Those who practice self-acceptance and self-compassion might become resilient and emotionally strong while dealing with inattention issues. It helps individuals to treat their ADHD symptoms with compassion, empathy, and a feeling of empowerment, which promotes improved self-worth and general wellbeing.

Chapter 3: Practical Techniques for Improving Focus and Attention

- **Mindfulness practices for enhancing attention and reducing distraction**
- **Incorporating meditation and relaxation techniques into daily routines**
- **Utilizing sensory strategies to promote focus and concentration**

Mindfulness practices for enhancing attention and reducing distraction

Mindfulness practices can be highly effective for enhancing attention and reducing distraction, especially for individuals managing ADHD symptoms. Here are some mindfulness techniques tailored to improve attention:

Focused Breathing: Sit comfortably and focus your attention on your breath. Notice the sensation of each inhale and exhale. When your mind starts to wander, gently bring your focus back to your breath without judgment.

Body Scan: Close your eyes and bring your attention to different parts of your body, starting from your toes and moving up to your head. Notice any sensations, tension, or areas of discomfort without trying to change anything. This practice helps to increase body awareness and bring attention into the present moment.

Mindful Observation: Choose an object in your environment, such as a flower, a candle flame, or a piece of artwork. Observe the object mindfully, noticing its colors, shapes, textures, and details. Allow yourself to fully immerse in the present moment experience without judgment or analysis.

Walking Meditation: Take a slow, deliberate walk, paying close attention to each step you take. Notice the sensations of your feet touching the ground, the movement of your body, and the surrounding environment. If your mind wanders, gently guide your attention back to the physical sensations of walking.

Mindful Eating: Engage in mindful eating by slowing down and savoring each bite of food. Notice the flavors, textures, and sensations of eating without distractions. Pay attention to your body's hunger and fullness cues, as well as the experience of nourishing your body.

Guided Meditation: Listen to guided meditation recordings that specifically focus on enhancing attention and reducing distraction. Follow along with the instructions provided by the meditation teacher, allowing yourself to relax and deepen your concentration.

Labeling Thoughts and Emotions: When distracting thoughts or emotions arise, practice labeling them without getting caught up in their content. Simply acknowledge them as "thinking" or "feeling" and gently return your attention to the present moment.

Mindful Technology Use: Practice mindfulness while using technology by setting intentional boundaries and being fully present with your devices. Take regular breaks to pause, breathe, and recenter your attention before continuing with your activities.

Consistent practice of mindfulness techniques can help strengthen attentional control, increase awareness of distracting thoughts and behaviors, and cultivate a greater sense of presence and focus in daily life. Integrating these practices into your routine can support your efforts to manage ADHD symptoms and enhance overall well-being.

Incorporating meditation and relaxation techniques into daily routines

For those managing symptoms of ADHD, including relaxation and meditation practices into daily routines may be quite helpful. Here are a few doable methods for incorporating these routines into your everyday life:

Start Small: To make meditation more approachable and less daunting, start with short meditation sessions, like five to ten minutes. You may progressively extend the time as you become more used to the exercise.

Select a Convenient Time: To include relaxation and meditation into your routine, determine the time of day that works best for you. It might be in the morning to concentrate and begin your day clearly, in the afternoon to take a break and refuel, or in the evening to relax and relieve tension.

Establish a Dedicated Space: Choose a peaceful, comfortable area in your house where you may meditate and unwind without interruptions. Arrange blankets, pillows, or a cozy chair to help with your posture and ease.

Try Out a Variety of Methods: Investigate several methods for relaxation and meditation to see which one(s) most suits you. This may include deep breathing techniques, yoga, gradual muscular relaxation, guided imagery, or mindfulness meditation.

Utilize applications and Recorded Meditations: Make use of internet guided meditation recordings and meditation applications. These sites include a large selection of guided sessions that may be customized to meet various time limits, skill levels, and preferences.

Include awareness in Daily Activities: Bring awareness to routine chores and activities like walking, eating, and dishwashing. As you go through these exercises, be mindful of your thoughts, feelings, and sensations in order to develop a stronger sense of awareness and present.

Establish Reminders and Schedules: Utilize your phone's or calendar's alarms and reminders to remind yourself to practice relaxation and meditation. Create a reliable timetable to help it become a regular aspect of your day.

Practice Breathing Exercises: To encourage relaxation and lower stress levels, include basic breathing exercises into your everyday routine. Throughout the day, take calm, deep breaths and pay attention to how the air feels entering and exiting your body.

Be Kind to Yourself: Approach relaxation techniques like meditation with a nonjudgmental, self-compassionate mindset. Give yourself permission to just be in the practice, without chasing after false goals or losing patience with your straying thoughts.

Take Note of the Advantages: Recognize the advantages of relaxing and meditation for your physical, mental, and emotional health. Throughout time, take note of any improvements in your level of attention, concentration, mood, and stress.

You may develop more calm, clarity, and resilience in the face of ADHD issues by including meditation and relaxation practices into your daily routines. This will improve your general quality of life.

Utilizing sensory strategies to promote focus and concentration

Utilizing sensory strategies can be an effective way to promote focus and concentration for adults managing ADHD symptoms. Here are several sensory strategies you can try:

Fidget Tools: Keep small, handheld fidget tools nearby during tasks that require concentration. Fidget spinners, stress balls, or textured objects can provide sensory stimulation and help channel excess energy, allowing for improved focus.

Chewable Items: Chewable necklaces, gum, or chewable pencils can provide sensory input and help individuals with ADHD maintain focus during tasks. Chewing can help regulate arousal levels and reduce restlessness.

Weighted Blankets or Lap Pads: Use weighted blankets or lap pads during seated activities to provide deep pressure stimulation, which can have a calming effect on the nervous system and promote relaxation and focus.

Noise-Canceling Headphones: Block out distracting noises in your environment with noise-canceling headphones or earplugs. Listen to instrumental music or white noise to create a calming auditory environment conducive to concentration.

Sensory Breaks: Incorporate short sensory breaks into your routine to prevent sensory overload and maintain focus. Take a brief walk, engage in stretching exercises, or spend a few minutes outdoors to refresh your senses and recharge your attention.

Sensory Diet Activities: Implement a sensory diet consisting of sensory-rich activities throughout the day to regulate arousal levels and promote optimal focus. Activities such as jumping on a mini-trampoline, swinging, or using therapy putty can provide proprioceptive and vestibular input to support attention.

Aromatherapy: Experiment with essential oils known for their calming and focusing properties, such as lavender, peppermint, or rosemary. Diffuse essential oils in your workspace or use a personal inhaler to benefit from their therapeutic effects.

Tactile Stimuli: Incorporate tactile stimuli into your environment to engage your sense of touch and promote focus. Use textured surfaces, such as a fidget mat or stress-relief toys with different textures, to provide tactile input and enhance sensory engagement.

Visual Organizers: Use visual organizers, such as color-coded calendars, task lists, or graphic organizers, to help structure information and improve visual attention. Break tasks into manageable steps and use visual cues to prioritize and organize activities.

Adjust Lighting: Optimize lighting conditions in your workspace to reduce visual distractions and eye strain. Use natural light whenever possible and adjust artificial lighting to minimize glare and shadows that may interfere with focus.

By incorporating sensory strategies into your daily routine, adults with ADHD can create a supportive environment that promotes focus, concentration, and productivity, ultimately enhancing their ability to manage tasks and responsibilities effectively.

Chapter 4: Time Management Strategies

- **Implementing effective time management tools and techniques**
- **Breaking tasks into smaller, manageable chunks**
- **Prioritizing tasks and managing deadlines to minimize inattention-related setbacks**

Implementing effective time management tools and techniques

Implementing effective time management tools and techniques is crucial for adults, especially those managing ADHD symptoms. Here are some strategies tailored to help adults improve their time management skills:

Use a Digital Calendar: Utilize digital calendar apps like Google Calendar, Outlook Calendar, or Apple Calendar to schedule appointments, deadlines, and tasks. Set reminders and notifications to stay on track and manage your time effectively.

Create To-Do Lists: Make daily or weekly to-do lists to prioritize tasks and track your progress. Break down large tasks into smaller, more manageable steps, and allocate specific time slots for each task on your list.

Prioritize Tasks: Identify tasks that are most important and time-sensitive, and prioritize them accordingly. Use techniques like the Eisenhower Matrix (urgent vs. important) to categorize tasks and focus on high-priority items first.

Set Realistic Goals: Establish realistic and achievable goals for each day, week, or month. Break goals into smaller milestones and celebrate your progress as you accomplish them.

Time Blocking: Allocate dedicated time blocks for specific activities or tasks throughout the day. Schedule uninterrupted periods for focused work, meetings, breaks, and personal activities, and stick to your planned schedule as much as possible.

Use Timers and Pomodoro Technique: Set timers to work in focused intervals, such as the Pomodoro Technique (25 minutes of focused work followed by a 5-minute break). This method can help improve productivity and maintain attention during tasks.

Batch Similar Tasks: Group similar tasks together and complete them in batches to minimize context switching and improve efficiency. For example, respond to emails, make phone calls, or complete administrative tasks during designated time blocks.

Limit Distractions: Identify and minimize distractions in your environment to maintain focus and productivity. Turn off notifications, silence your phone, and use website blockers or apps to restrict access to distracting websites or social media platforms during work periods.

Review and Reflect: Regularly review your progress, assess your time management strategies, and identify areas for improvement. Reflect on what worked well and what could be adjusted to enhance your efficiency and effectiveness.

Seek Accountability and Support: Share your goals and time management strategies with a trusted friend, colleague, or mentor who can provide accountability and support. Consider joining productivity groups or seeking professional guidance if you need additional assistance.

By implementing these time management tools and techniques, adults can enhance their productivity, reduce procrastination, and better manage their time to achieve their personal and professional goals effectively.

Breaking tasks into smaller, manageable chunks

Breaking tasks into smaller, manageable chunks is an effective strategy for adults, especially those managing ADHD symptoms. Here's how to break tasks down effectively:

Define the Task: Clearly define the task or goal you want to accomplish. Be specific about what needs to be done and why it's important.

Identify Subtasks: Break the main task down into smaller, more manageable subtasks or steps. Think about the sequence of actions required to complete the task successfully.

Set Milestones: Identify key milestones or checkpoints along the way to monitor your progress. Break the task into stages and set deadlines for completing each stage.

Prioritize Subtasks: Determine the order of priority for each subtask based on urgency, importance, or dependencies. Focus on completing high-priority subtasks first to make progress toward your overall goal.

Estimate Time and Effort: Estimate the time and effort required to complete each subtask realistically. Consider factors such as complexity, resources needed, and potential challenges.

Allocate Resources: Ensure you have the necessary resources, tools, and support to complete each subtask effectively. Allocate time, energy, and resources accordingly to prevent overwhelm and burnout.

Break Down Complex Tasks: If a task feels overwhelming or complex, break it down into smaller, more manageable components. Divide the task into logical segments that can be tackled individually.

Use Visual Aids: Visualize your task breakdown using diagrams, mind maps, or flowcharts to help you visualize the sequence of steps and dependencies involved.

Focus on One Subtask at a Time: Avoid multitasking and focus on completing one subtask at a time. By concentrating your attention and energy on one task, you can maintain focus and productivity more effectively.

Celebrate Progress: Celebrate your achievements and progress as you complete each subtask. Acknowledge your efforts and give yourself credit for the milestones you've reached along the way.

Review and Adjust: Regularly review your task breakdown and adjust your plan as needed based on changing priorities, obstacles, or new information. Be flexible and willing to adapt your approach as circumstances evolve.

Breaking tasks into smaller, manageable chunks helps adults with ADHD overcome feelings of overwhelm, increase motivation, and maintain focus and productivity. By breaking tasks down into actionable steps, individuals can make progress toward their goals more effectively and with less stress.

Prioritizing tasks and managing deadlines to minimize inattention-related setbacks

Prioritizing tasks and managing deadlines effectively is essential for minimizing inattention-related setbacks in adults, especially those managing ADHD symptoms. Here's how to prioritize tasks and manage deadlines effectively:

Make a List of Tasks: Start by listing all the tasks you need to accomplish. Include both short-term and long-term tasks, as well as any deadlines associated with each task.

Assess Task Importance and Urgency: Evaluate the importance and urgency of each task. Consider factors such as deadlines, consequences of not completing the task on time, and impact on your overall goals and priorities.

Use Prioritization Techniques: Employ prioritization techniques such as the Eisenhower Matrix, ABCDE method, or the 1-2-3 method to categorize tasks based on their level of importance and urgency. Focus on completing high-priority tasks first.

Break Down Complex Tasks: If a task seems overwhelming or complex, break it down into smaller, more manageable subtasks. Prioritize the subtasks based on their importance and urgency, and tackle them one at a time.

Consider Time and Resources: Take into account the time and resources required to complete each task. Allocate sufficient time and resources to high-priority tasks to ensure they are completed effectively and on time.

Set Realistic Deadlines: Set realistic deadlines for each task based on its complexity and importance. Avoid overcommitting yourself and be mindful of your capacity to complete tasks within the given time frame.

Use Visual Tools: Use visual tools such as calendars, planners, or digital task management apps to keep track of deadlines and prioritize tasks visually. Color-coding or labeling tasks can help you identify priorities at a glance.

Break Down Time Blocks: Allocate dedicated time blocks for specific tasks or categories of tasks throughout the day. Schedule focused work periods interspersed with short breaks to maintain productivity and prevent burnout.

Limit Distractions: Minimize distractions in your environment to stay focused and productive during work periods. Turn off notifications, set boundaries with colleagues or family members, and create a conducive workspace for concentration.

Review and Adjust Regularly: Regularly review your task list and deadlines to ensure you are staying on track. Adjust your priorities and deadlines as needed based on changing circumstances, new information, or shifting priorities.

Celebrate Progress: Celebrate your accomplishments and progress as you complete tasks and meet deadlines. Recognize your efforts and give yourself credit for achieving your goals, no matter how small.

By prioritizing tasks and managing deadlines effectively, adults with ADHD can minimize inattention-related setbacks, increase productivity, and achieve their goals more efficiently. Consistent practice and refinement of time management skills can lead to improved focus, reduced stress, and greater overall success in managing tasks and responsibilities.

Chapter 5: Organizational Systems and Solutions

- Creating an organized environment conducive to productivity
- Implementing organizational tools such as planners, calendars, and task lists
- Establishing routines and systems to streamline daily tasks and responsibilities

Creating an organized environment conducive to productivity

Adults need to make sure their workspace is organized in order to be productive, particularly if they are also managing symptoms of ADHD. Here are various methods to make this happen:

Declutter Your Space: Make your surroundings clutter-free first. To establish a clear and organized workplace that encourages attention and clarity, clear out any extraneous things, papers, and clutter.

Assign Particular Work Areas: Set aside particular spaces in your house or place of business for various tasks. Establish a designated location for work-related duties, a different room for leisure or relaxation, and a third place for home chores.

Invest in Storage Solutions: To keep your possessions properly arranged and conveniently accessible, invest in storage solutions like shelves, cabinets, bins, and organizers. Sort and arrange objects according to kind or purpose using labels and storage containers.

Establish a Filing method: Create a method for organizing papers, documents, and crucial data. Files should be arranged into folders or categories according to their importance and use. For simple retrieval, think about using digital filing systems or color-coded labeling.

Employ Clear and Visible signs: To help you remember critical tasks or deadlines, use labels, clear and visible signs, or visual cues to indicate where objects go. Display to-do lists and reminders using whiteboards, bulletin boards, or sticky notes.

Create Daily Routines: To keep your daily activities organized and structured, create daily routines and habits. Allocate certain periods for doing chores, working, cleaning, exercising, and unwinding.

Reduce Distractions: Recognize possible sources of distraction in your surroundings and take action to reduce them. Establish boundaries with family members or roommates during concentrated work hours, restrict access to websites and applications that might be distracting, and wear noise-canceling headphones to drown out background sounds.

Establish a Functional workstation: Arrange your workstation to maximize comfort and efficiency. Select ergonomic furniture, make sure your workstation is well-ventilated and favorable to focus, and adjust lighting to prevent glare.

Establish a Daily Cleanup Routine: Set aside some time each day to organize your workstation and prepare it for the next day. To keep a place tidy and clutter-free, put things away, file paperwork, and clean surfaces.

Remain Both Flexible and Consistent: Remain both flexible and ready to make necessary system adaptations while maintaining consistency in your organizational efforts. Evaluate what's functioning properly and what needs improvement on a regular basis, then make the necessary modifications.

Adults may avoid distractions, decrease stress, and maximize their ability to concentrate and complete activities efficiently by setting up an orderly workspace that promotes productivity. The regular use of these techniques may result in enhanced productivity, clarity, and general well-being in one's personal and professional life.

Implementing organizational tools such as planners, calendars, and task lists

Using calendars, planners, and task lists is essential for adults, especially those who are managing symptoms of ADHD. Here's how to use these tools efficiently:

Pick the Correct Tools: Make sure the organizing tools you choose fit your needs, tastes, and way of life. Select tools that fit your organizing style and those you feel comfortable using, whether it's a digital calendar, paper planner, or task management software.

Consolidate Information: To ensure everything is readily available and to prevent confusion, consolidate your projects, appointments, and deadlines into one location. To collect and arrange all pertinent data, use the organizing tools you have selected.

Note Significant Dates and Deadlines: Keep a note of significant dates, deadlines, appointments, and activities in your calendar. Add all of your obligations, both personal and professional, to get a complete picture of your calendar.

Divide Larger jobs into Manageable pieces: Utilize your planner or task list to divide more complex jobs into smaller, more manageable pieces. Prioritize your tasks according to their urgency and significance, then list the precise steps you must take to accomplish each one.

Set Reasonable Objectives and Deadlines: Give each work or project a reasonable set of objectives and a deadline. Recognize your limits and refrain from taking on more than you can handle. Establish realistic deadlines that will give you enough time to do projects without feeling overburdened.

Employ Visual Cues and Reminders: To help you visually distinguish between tasks and priorities in your planner or calendar, use color-coding, stickers, or symbols. To help you remember key dates and appointments, set alarms and reminders.

Review and Update Frequently: Develop the practice of routinely reviewing and updating your tools for organizing. Make sure you are informed of forthcoming obligations and duties by regularly reviewing your calendar and to-do list. Make any necessary updates to your plans in light of new knowledge or shifting priorities.

Task Prioritization: Sort jobs according to their urgency and significance. Classify jobs using methods such as the Eisenhower Matrix or the ABCDE approach, and give precedence to the highest-priority things first.

Plan Dedicated Work Blocks: Set aside certain times in your schedule for productive and concentrated work. Set aside undisturbed time to do work that calls for intense focus, and try to avoid arranging appointments or other obligations during this time.

Celebrate Your Progress: As you finish chores and reach milestones, acknowledge and celebrate your successes. Give yourself credit for your efforts and for maintaining your organization and productivity.

Adults may improve time management, task prioritization, and commitment management by using organizing tools like calendars, planners, and task lists. Using these tools on a regular basis may boost output, lower stress levels, and enhance general organization in both personal and professional life.

Establishing routines and systems to streamline daily tasks and responsibilities

For adults, particularly those who are managing symptoms of ADHD, creating routines and procedures to simplify everyday activities and obligations is critically important. The following techniques may be used to establish efficient routines and systems:

Establish Priorities: Start by determining your objectives and top priorities. Ascertain the duties and obligations that have the most significance for you, both in the immediate and distant future.

Divide Work: Divide more ambitious projects and objectives into smaller, more doable stages. As a result, they are less daunting and simpler to deal with on a daily basis.

Make a calendar: Decide when you will devote your attention to certain jobs and activities. Make a daily or weekly calendar. To remember appointments, due dates, and recurring obligations, use a planner, calendar, or digital scheduling tool.

Set Aside Time Blocks: Assign specific time slots for several types of duties, including work, housework, exercise, and recreational activities. Setting out time for each task promotes organization and guarantees that all priorities are met.

Create Morning and Evening Routines: To round off the day, create reliable morning and evening routines. Incorporate routines like getting up at the same time every day, making a plan for the day, going over your assignments, relaxing before bed, and getting ready for the following day.

Employ Organizational Tools: To stay on top of assignments and due dates, make use of tools for organization including calendars, task lists, planners, and reminder applications. Whether they are digital or paper-based, choose tools that fit your needs and style.

Task Prioritization: Sort jobs according to their urgency and significance. Prioritize finishing high-priority projects first, and provide enough time and resources to guarantee their efficient completion.

Put Checklists into Practice: To make sure nothing is missed, make checklists for routines or recurrent chores. You can prevent forgetfulness, remain organized, and keep your daily activities consistent by using checklists.

Evaluate and Think: Evaluate your processes and procedures on a regular basis to see how successful they are. To maximize your workflow, consider what is going well and what may be better. Then, make the necessary modifications.

Remain Adaptable: Although routines and procedures provide structure, it's crucial to maintain your flexibility and adaptability. Be willing to adjust when conditions and priorities change.

Exercise Self-Compassion: As you create and improve your routines and processes, have patience and compassion for yourself. Acknowledge that finding what works best for you can take some time, and be prepared to try different things and make adjustments as you go.

Adults may decrease stress, boost productivity, and simplify everyday activities and obligations by putting in place efficient routines and procedures. Success in both the personal and professional spheres depends on balance and a combination of consistency, organization, and adaptability.

Chapter 6: Minimizing Distractions and Enhancing Environment

- **Identifying common sources of distraction in daily life**
- **Implementing strategies to reduce environmental distractions**
- **Creating a conducive workspace for improved focus and productivity**

Identifying common sources of distraction in daily life

Identifying common sources of distraction in daily life is crucial for developing strategies to manage attention and improve focus. Here are some common sources of distraction:

Digital Devices: Smartphones, tablets, and computers can be significant sources of distraction due to notifications, social media, emails, and other apps that constantly vie for attention.

Social Media: Platforms like Facebook, Instagram, Twitter, and TikTok are designed to be engaging and addictive, making it easy to lose track of time and focus when scrolling through feeds or engaging with content.

Email and Messaging Apps: Constant email alerts, text messages, and instant messaging platforms can interrupt workflow and divert attention away from important tasks.

Multitasking: Attempting to juggle multiple tasks simultaneously can lead to decreased focus and productivity. Multitasking often results in divided attention and reduced effectiveness in completing tasks.

Environmental Distractions: Noise, interruptions from colleagues or family members, clutter, and disorganization in the physical environment can all contribute to distractions and hinder concentration.

Procrastination: Putting off tasks or delaying important responsibilities can lead to increased stress and anxiety, as well as a loss of focus when deadlines loom closer.

Inner Thoughts and Worries: Internal distractions such as intrusive thoughts, worries, and anxieties about past or future events can occupy mental space and interfere with concentration on present tasks.

Lack of Structure or Routine: A lack of structure or routine in daily life can make it difficult to maintain focus and stay on track with tasks and responsibilities.

Physical Discomfort: Discomfort from hunger, thirst, fatigue, or discomfort from an uncomfortable workspace can detract from focus and productivity.

Overstimulation: Exposure to excessive stimuli, such as bright lights, loud noises, or crowded environments, can overwhelm the senses and make it challenging to concentrate.

Task Switching: Constantly switching between tasks or being pulled in multiple directions can disrupt workflow and impede progress on important tasks.

Identifying these common sources of distraction can help individuals develop strategies to minimize their impact and create an environment conducive to focus and productivity. By recognizing and addressing distractions proactively, individuals can improve their ability to concentrate and achieve their goals effectively.

Implementing strategies to reduce environmental distractions

Putting techniques in place to lessen outside distractions may greatly increase productivity and attention. Here are a few successful tactics:

Establish a Dedicated Workspace: Make a location for yourself that is favorable to concentration and free from interruptions. Assemble your workplace with all the required equipment and supplies in a peaceful location with little foot traffic and clutter.

Reduce Noise: To reduce noise distractions, use earplugs to filter out background noise, white noise machines, or noise-canceling headphones. As an alternative, turn to background noise or instrumental music to aid with attention and focus.

Establish limits: To reduce distractions while work or concentrated tasks, establish limits with family members, roommates, or coworkers.

Declare clearly when you are unable to be contacted and express your desire for privacy.

Control Digital Distractions: To reduce interruptions from emails, social media, and other applications, turn off not-so-essential alerts on your electronic devices. To prevent access to websites that might be distracting while working, use applications or browser extensions.

Organize and Declutter: To reduce visual distractions, maintain an orderly and clutter-free environment. To keep goods neatly and out of sight, use storage options like shelves, drawers, and containers.

Establish Boundaries for Your Work Hours: Decide in advance what times you will work, take breaks, and spend time with family and friends. Try your best to stick to your routine in order to keep things consistent and reduce outside distractions.

Use Visual Cues: To let others know when you are in concentrate mode and shouldn't be bothered, use visual cues like closed doors, signs, or symbols. Discuss the importance of these signals with people in your home or place of business.

Use relaxation and mindfulness techniques: To help you concentrate and manage stress, include mindfulness and relaxation practices into your everyday routine. To quiet the mind and cut down on distractions, try progressive muscle relaxation, deep breathing, or meditation.

Plan Regular Breaks: Throughout your workday, set aside time to relax, rejuvenate, and concentrate. In order to avoid burnout and preserve productivity, take advantage of break moments to stretch, drink water, or do quick relaxation techniques.

Modify Lighting: To lessen eye strain and tiredness, optimize the lighting in your workstation. When feasible, utilize natural light;

when not, use artificial lighting to reduce glare and shadows that might be distracting.

By putting these tactics into practice, you may establish a setting that encourages concentration, output, and wellbeing, which will help you do jobs more quickly and skillfully.

Creating a conducive workspace for improved focus and productivity

Establishing a workplace that promotes increased attention and productivity is crucial for adults, particularly those who are managing symptoms of ADHD. The following advice may help you set up the ideal workspace:

Pick the Perfect Spot: Make your workstation peaceful and somewhat private in your house or place of business. It should ideally be far from busy streets and other sources of distraction.

Organize and declutter: Maintain a clean, organized, and clutter-free workstation. Eliminate extraneous objects and documents that may cause distractions and visual disarray. To arrange supplies and materials, make use of storage options including shelves, drawers, and containers.

Optimize Ergonomics: To encourage proper posture and avoid pain or strain, make an investment in ergonomic furniture and equipment. Select a chair that is comfortable and provides enough back support, set your computer display so that it is at eye level, and use a mouse and keyboard that let you move your arms and wrists freely.

Control Lighting: Make sure your work area has enough natural or artificial lighting to improve vision and lessen eye strain. To optimize natural light, place your workstation next to windows. When necessary, use adjustable task lighting to supplement ambient light.

Reduce Distractions: Examine your workstation for possible sources of distraction and take action to reduce them. Set limits with family members or coworkers to reduce interruptions, and use white noise generators or noise-canceling headphones to drown out annoying noises.

Customize Your Space: Add motivational and inspiring objects to your desk to make it uniquely yours. Put phrases, images, or works of art on display that make you feel better and uplifted. Select décor that is a reflection of your tastes and personality.

Organize Tools and materials: To reduce interruptions and preserve production, keep commonly used tools and materials close to hand. To keep pens, paper, files, and other necessities organized, use desktop organizers, trays, and caddies.

Make Zones for Various Activities: Set aside separate areas of your workstation for different tasks, such as using a computer for work, a writing desk for planning or brainstorming, and a cozy reclining area for unwinding or reading.

Create Rituals and Routines: Create rituals and schedules to indicate the beginning and conclusion of workdays. Develop routines that include arranging your workplace neatly at the end of the day, going over your priorities and plan first thing in the morning, and taking frequent breaks to stretch and recharge.

Invest in Tech Tools: Organize your workplace and increase productivity by using tech tools and applications. To remain organized and remember deadlines and obligations, think about using digital calendars, note-taking tools, and task management applications.

Even while treating the symptoms of ADHD, you may optimize your surroundings for success and efficiently handle activities and obligations by setting up a workplace that encourages attention, organization, and productivity.

Chapter 7: Strategies for Improving Memory and Recall

- **Techniques for enhancing memory and recall in individuals with ADHD**
- **Utilizing mnemonic devices and memory aids to improve retention**
- **Incorporating memory-boosting activities and exercises into daily routines**

Techniques for enhancing memory and recall in individuals with ADHD

For those with ADHD, improving memory and recall may be especially helpful since it can aid with attention, organization, and general cognitive function. Here are some methods designed to help individuals with ADHD with their memory and recall:

Employ Visual Aids: You may arrange information in a more aesthetically pleasing and memorable manner by using visual aids like charts, diagrams, mind maps, and color-coded lists. When necessary, visual cues might help to prompt memory recall.

Chunking Information: Information should be divided into more digestible, smaller sections or categories. To help with memory and recall, group similar objects together and arrange them in a systematic manner.

Employ Mnemonic Devices: Mnemonic devices may aid in the more efficient encoding and retrieval of information. Examples of these devices include acronyms, rhymes, and visual images. To make the material you need to remember more remembered and interesting, come up with mnemonic devices that are related to it.

Repetition and Review: To strengthen memory retention, engage in active repetition and review of the material. Repeatedly going over content at different intervals helps improve memory consolidation and recall.

Use Several Senses: When learning and studying material, use a variety of senses. To improve memory encoding and retrieval, include kinesthetic, visual, and aural components in your learning process.

Establish linkages and links: Make links and linkages between recently acquired knowledge and prior experiences or knowledge. To aid in memory recall, make mental connections between disparate bits of information or relate new thoughts to well-known notions.

Employ Memory Aids: To help you remember key facts and cues, make use of memory aids like voice memos, voice memo sticks, digital reminders, or smartphone applications. In order to assist internal memory operations, these instruments may act as external memory supports.

Practice awareness and attention: When engaging in learning and memory exercises, cultivate awareness and attention. Reduce distractions and improve focus by engaging in mindfulness exercises like progressive muscle relaxation, deep breathing, or meditation.

Divide Up the Work into Doable Steps: Divide up mentally taxing activities into smaller, more doable segments. Keep moving forward by concentrating on finishing one task at a time and tracking your progress using checklists or visual indicators.

Get Enough Sleep and Exercise: Since sleep and exercise are essential for memory consolidation and cognitive performance, give them top priority. To promote general brain health, try to get enough sleep every night and engage in regular exercise.

Seek Professional Assistance: To receive individualized methods and approaches catered to your unique requirements and issues, think about consulting with a mental health professional or ADHD coach.

Adults with ADHD may improve learning outcomes, increase memory and recall, and efficiently manage cognitive activities and responsibilities in all facets of life by putting these ideas and practices into practice.

Utilizing mnemonic devices and memory aids to improve retention

Utilizing mnemonic devices and memory aids can significantly improve retention, especially for individuals with ADHD. Here are some effective techniques:

Acronyms and Acrostics: Create acronyms or acrostics to remember lists or sequences of information. For example, to remember the order of the planets in our solar system: "My Very Educated Mother Just Served Us Noodles" (Mercury, Venus, Earth, Mars, Jupiter, Saturn, Uranus, Neptune).

Rhymes and Songs: Create rhymes or songs to help remember information. Turning facts into catchy tunes or rhymes can make them easier to recall. For example, "Thirty days hath September, April, June, and November" helps remember the number of days in each month.

Visualization: Visualize vivid images or scenes associated with the information you want to remember. The more absurd or unusual the image, the more memorable it tends to be. Visual associations can help trigger recall more effectively.

Memory Palaces: Use the method of loci or memory palace technique, where you mentally place items you want to remember in specific locations in a familiar space, such as your home. As you mentally walk through the space, you recall the items associated with each location.

Chunking: Break down large amounts of information into smaller, more manageable chunks. Group related items together and organize them into meaningful categories to facilitate memory retrieval.

Association: Create associations between new information and familiar concepts or experiences. Relate new facts or ideas to something you already know, making it easier to recall when needed.

Color Coding: Use color coding to organize and differentiate information. Assign specific colors to categories or concepts, making it easier to visually distinguish and remember key details.

Memory Aids: Use memory aids such as sticky notes, digital reminders, voice recordings, or smartphone apps to capture important information and cues. These tools serve as external memory supports to supplement internal memory processes.

Mind Maps: Create visual mind maps to visually organize and connect ideas or concepts. Mind maps help visualize relationships between information and aid in memory retrieval by providing a structured overview of the topic.

Repetition and Review: Practice active repetition and review of information to reinforce memory retention. Review material multiple times over spaced intervals to strengthen memory recall and consolidation.

By incorporating mnemonic devices and memory aids into your learning and recall strategies, you can improve retention, enhance learning outcomes, and effectively manage cognitive tasks and responsibilities. Experiment with different techniques to find the ones that work best for you.

Incorporating memory-boosting activities and exercises into daily routines

Including memory-enhancing exercises and activities in everyday routines may be quite helpful for adults, especially those who are managing symptoms of ADHD. The following are some practical methods to enhance cognitive function and memory retention:

Games: Play games and puzzles that exercise the brain, such as Sudoku, word puzzles, logic puzzles, crosswords, and brain-training applications. These mental exercises strain your brain and improve memory among other cognitive abilities.

Learn Something New: To improve memory retention and brain stimulation, pick up a new activity, skill, or language. Acquiring new knowledge and abilities fortifies preexisting brain networks and forms new ones, enhancing cognitive performance overall.

Practice Visualization: To improve memory recall, engage in visualization activities. Conjure up vivid pictures or scenarios that are connected to the knowledge you want to retain. The effectiveness of imagery for memory recall increases with its level of detail and vividness.

Mindfullness and Meditation: Improve your concentration, attention span, and memory by including mindfulness meditation into your everyday practice. Engaging in mindfulness activities may lower stress, improve cognitive performance, and support mental health in general.

Physical Activity: Studies have shown that regular physical activity enhances memory retention and cognitive performance. Take part in aerobic workouts that improve brain health and increase blood flow to the brain, such as cycling, running, swimming, or walking.

Get Enough Sleep: To enhance memory consolidation and cognitive performance, make high-quality sleep a priority. Try to get between seven and nine hours of sleep every night to give your brain enough time to properly absorb and remember knowledge.

Practice Retrieval Strategies: To improve memory retention, practice retrieval strategies including active recall and self-testing. To help with learning and retention, test yourself on material you've just learnt or attempt to remember important specifics.

Chunking and Organization: Divide information into more digestible, smaller pieces and arrange them in a methodical manner. Utilize visual aids or mnemonic devices in conjunction with grouping similar information to help with memory recall and retention.

Keep a Healthy Diet: Consume a well-balanced diet full of nutrients that are known to improve brain function, such as antioxidants, vitamins, minerals, and omega-3 fatty acids. Nuts, seeds, fruits, vegetables, whole grains, and fatty fish are foods that promote brain health and cognitive performance.

Maintain Social Connectivity: Maintain social connections with friends, family, and peers by participating in meaningful social interactions. Participating in social activities improves memory retention, boosts cognitive function, and supports mental wellness in general.

Reduce Stress: Use relaxation methods to control your stress, such progressive muscle relaxation, yoga, meditation, and deep breathing. It's important to have good coping mechanisms for stress since prolonged stress might impede memory and cognitive performance.

You may strengthen cognitive function, maintain general brain health, and increase memory recall by including these memory-boosting workouts and activities into your daily routine. Try out a variety of tactics to see which ones work best for you, then include them into your daily routine.

Chapter 8: Building Support Networks and Seeking Professional Help

- Seeking support from friends, family, and peers in managing inattention challenges
- Exploring the role of therapy and coaching in addressing inattention symptoms
- Seeking professional guidance and resources for comprehensive ADHD management

Seeking support from friends, family, and peers in managing inattention challenges

Getting help from classmates, family, and friends may be very helpful in managing inattention issues, particularly for those who have ADHD. Here are a few methods for asking for and getting help:

Open Communication: Discuss your inattention issues and how they impact your day-to-day activities with your friends, family, and peers in an honest and open manner. Tell us about any particular tactics or modifications that have improved your ability to control your symptoms.

Educate Others: Share information on ADHD, its symptoms, and its effects on your life with others in your support system. Assist them in realizing that attention, concentration, and executive function are all impacted by ADHD, a neurodevelopmental disease.

Set Reasonable Expectations: Be honest with your loved ones about your capabilities and constraints. Make it clear to them that you may need extra assistance or accommodations in order to complete certain jobs or circumstances.

Determine Your Specific Needs: Determine the precise areas in which you may need help or support. Tell your support system how they can assist you most, whether it's by sending you appointment reminders, organizing your life, or just being there to listen.

Create Routines and Structures: To keep yourself organized and on track, collaborate with your peers, family, and friends to create routines and structures. This might include establishing a routine for studying, socializing, or doing duties around the home.

Promote Positive Reinforcement: Promote positive reinforcement and acknowledge your achievements and hard work. Together, celebrate little accomplishments and benchmarks, and acknowledge the strides you're making in overcoming your inattentional problems.

Establish a Supportive Environment: Try to surround yourself with people who are sympathetic and supportive, since this will help you accept and empathize with others. Look for relatives, friends, or support groups where you can talk about your struggles and experiences without feeling awkward.

Include Others in Goal creating: Include the people in your support system in conversations about creating goals and addressing problems. Together, establish reasonable objectives and plans of action, and solicit advice and comments as you proceed.

Engage in Empathy and Active Listening: When engaging with your support system, engage in empathy and active listening. Thank them for their cooperation and understanding, and be open to hearing about their thoughts and worries.

Seek Professional Help Together: You may want to think about enrolling members of your support system in ADHD-focused therapy sessions or educational programs. Participating in therapy or support groups as a group helps promote empathy, communication, and common coping mechanisms.

Those with ADHD may create a strong network of understanding and support by asking friends, family, and peers for help. Together, you can overcome obstacles, recognize accomplishments, and create an atmosphere that encourages tolerance, resiliency, and development.

Exploring the role of therapy and coaching in addressing inattention symptoms

Therapy and coaching can play valuable roles in addressing inattention symptoms, especially for individuals with ADHD. Here's how each can help:

Therapy (Counseling or Psychotherapy):

Cognitive Behavioral Therapy (CBT): CBT can help individuals with ADHD identify and challenge negative thought patterns, develop coping strategies for managing inattention symptoms, and improve executive functioning skills.

Mindfulness-Based Therapy: Mindfulness-based approaches, such as Mindfulness-Based Cognitive Therapy (MBCT) or Mindfulness-Based Stress Reduction (MBSR), can help individuals with ADHD develop greater awareness of their thoughts and emotions, reduce stress, and enhance attention and focus.

Behavior Therapy: Behavior therapy focuses on modifying behaviors associated with ADHD symptoms, such as impulsivity and inattention. It involves setting specific goals, implementing behavioral interventions, and monitoring progress over time.

Family Therapy: Family therapy can help improve communication, understanding, and support within the family unit. It provides a safe space for family members to discuss challenges related to ADHD and develop effective coping strategies together.

Coaching:

ADHD Coaching: ADHD coaching is a specialized form of coaching designed to support individuals with ADHD in managing symptoms, improving executive functioning skills, and achieving personal and professional goals. Coaches provide accountability, structure, and practical strategies tailored to the individual's unique needs.

Executive Functioning Coaching: Executive functioning coaches focus on improving specific skills related to planning, organization, time management, prioritization, and task initiation. They help individuals with ADHD develop strategies to overcome challenges and succeed in various areas of life.

Career Coaching: Career coaches work with individuals with ADHD to explore career interests, set career goals, overcome obstacles in the workplace, and develop strategies for managing ADHD-related challenges in professional settings.

Life Coaching: Life coaches help individuals with ADHD clarify their values, set meaningful goals, and make positive changes in various aspects of life, such as relationships, health, finances, and personal development.

Therapy and coaching can be used individually or in combination to address inattention symptoms and improve overall functioning. It's important for individuals with ADHD to work with qualified professionals who have experience and expertise in treating ADHD and related challenges. By exploring therapy and coaching options, individuals with ADHD can gain valuable support, learn effective coping strategies, and enhance their quality of life.

Seeking professional guidance and resources for comprehensive ADHD management

In order to successfully handle the issues associated with ADHD, it is vital to seek expert help and resources for complete ADHD treatment. Here are some important experts and sources to think about:

Psychologists and psychiatrists: These professionals are experts in the diagnosis and treatment of ADHD and other associated mental health issues. To treat the symptoms of ADHD, they might do thorough assessments, provide medication, and give counseling or psychotherapy.

ADHD Specialists: You should think about obtaining therapy from medical experts that specialize in the diagnosis and management of ADHD. Developmental pediatricians, psychologists, neurologists, psychiatrists, and psychiatrists with training in ADHD screening and treatment are examples of ADHD specialists.

Counselors and therapists: Counselors and therapists may provide psychotherapy or counseling to treat co-occurring mental health issues including depression or anxiety, enhance coping mechanisms, and address symptoms of ADHD. In the treatment of ADHD, cognitive-behavioral therapy (CBT) and mindfulness-based techniques are often used.

ADHD Coaches: ADHD coaches are experts in helping people with ADHD create plans for symptom management, enhancing executive functioning, and accomplishing both personal and professional objectives. They provide responsibility, assistance, and useful resources that are customized to meet the requirements of the person.

Support Groups: Associating with ADHD support groups may provide beneficial peer assistance, useful guidance, and motivation from others who comprehend the difficulties of managing ADHD. Numerous support groups provide chances for experience sharing, knowledge sharing, and community building, whether they are held in person or virtually.

Educational Resources: To assist people with ADHD and their families learn more about the illness and create practical symptom management plans, a plethora of books, websites, podcasts, and other online resources are accessible. Seek for reliable information sites that have been approved by groups that support ADHD advocacy or medical experts.

ADHD Advocacy Groups and Organizations: The Attention Deficit Disorder Association (ADDDA) and Children and Adults with Attention-Deficit/Hyperactivity Disorder (CHADD) are two organizations that provide persons with ADHD and their families a wealth of information, support, and education. They provide local chapters, publications, webinars, conferences, and other ways for you to network and learn about managing ADHD.

Parent Education Programs: Parent education programs, like the Incredible Years program or Parent-Child Interaction Therapy (PCIT), can give parents of children with ADHD useful skills and strategies for behavior management, enhancing parent-child communication, and building healthy relationships.

Online Therapy Platforms: Take into consideration using online therapy platforms that provide access to counselors and qualified therapists with expertise in treating ADHD. These platforms often provide practical and reasonably priced ways to get counseling and assistance without leaving the comforts of your home.

To address the complex nature of ADHD, it's critical to collaborate with medical specialists and use a variety of treatment techniques. Individuals and families may improve overall quality of life and cope with symptoms more effectively by looking for complete ADHD treatment options and assistance.

Conclusion: Thriving with Inattention

- **Reflecting on progress and growth in managing inattention challenges**
- **Embracing a positive mindset and resilience in the face of setbacks**
- **Looking towards the future with optimism and confidence in one's ability to thrive with ADHD**

Reflecting on progress and growth in managing inattention challenges

It may be beneficial for people with ADHD to reflect on their development and success in handling inattention issues. This can help them celebrate their progress toward improved self-management, discover areas for growth, and acknowledge their triumphs. When thinking back on development and growth, keep the following important points in mind:

Identify Successes: Evaluate your level of success in handling your inattention issues. Think back on certain successes, no matter how little they may appear, including finishing projects on schedule, trying out novel tactics, or being more focused and productive.

Acknowledge work and Persistence: Give yourself credit for the work and tenacity you've put into controlling your inattentional problems. Recognize the efforts you've made to educate yourself about ADHD, look for assistance, and put coping mechanisms into practice to enhance your day-to-day functioning.

Celebrate Your Successes: Acknowledge and honor your accomplishments along the road. Take time to recognize and celebrate your accomplishments, whether they be achieving a personal goal, getting over a specific challenge, or making progress in symptom management.

Learn from Setbacks: Consider the difficulties and setbacks you've had to deal with while trying to manage your symptoms of inattention. Make the most of these experiences as a chance to develop and learn, and think about what tactics or changes may make it easier for you to deal with similar circumstances in the future.

Exercise Self-Compassion: Treat yourself with kindness while you consider your development and advancement. Acknowledge that obstacles are a normal part of the path and that handling inattention issues may be difficult. Treat yourself with patience, tolerance, and acceptance as you cultivate self-compassion.

Set Reasonable Expectations: Be reasonable with yourself and your ability to handle inattention issues. Recognize that growth may not always be straight-line and that having good and bad days is OK. Pay attention to long-term, consistent development and progress.

Honor Personal Development: Consider how handling your attention issues has aided in your own development. Think about how managing your everyday life with ADHD has made you more resourceful, resilient, and adaptive.

Seek Support and Feedback: Consult dependable family members, friends, or medical experts for their opinions on how well you are handling your inattention issues. Along the way, their viewpoints and thoughts may provide a great deal of support, affirmation, and direction.

Establish New Objectives: After considering your development and progress, establish new objectives and ambitions for yourself. Decide what areas you want to keep getting better in and make a list of attainable objectives to help you manage your inattention issues.

Above all, remember to enjoy the progress you've experienced and the journey you've taken in managing your inattention difficulties. Accept the highs and lows, achievements and failures, and acknowledge the fortitude and bravery you've shown in overcoming the difficulties brought on by ADHD.

People with ADHD may develop important insights, self-awareness, and a feeling of empowerment and resilience in their path towards better self-management and well-being by reflecting on their progress and improvement in managing inattention difficulties.

Embracing a positive mindset and resilience in the face of setbacks

It is crucial to have a positive outlook and demonstrate perseverance when faced with obstacles, particularly for those coping with inattention disorders like ADHD. The following are some techniques to develop resilience and an optimistic mindset:

Practice thanks: Develop an attitude of thankfulness by highlighting your life's blessings and expressing your thanks for what you have. Maintain a gratitude diary or set aside some time every day to think back on and express your thanks for the things that make you happy and fulfilled.

Concentrate on Your Strengths: Acknowledge and honor your abilities, successes, and strengths. Instead of concentrating on your flaws or failures, change your attention to your strengths and room for improvement.

Challenge Negative ideas: Change your perspective to one that is more realistic and optimistic in order to combat negative ideas and self-doubt. Use cognitive restructuring strategies to swap out your negative self-talk with powerful and reassuring ideas.

Create Coping Mechanisms: Determine the mechanisms that enable you to deal with obstacles and disappointments in a successful manner. Investigate stress-reduction tactics, mindfulness exercises, and relaxation methods to increase resilience and handle hardship.

Seek Support: In trying times, turn to friends, family, or support groups for words of wisdom, encouragement, and affirmation. Embrace a network of encouraging and motivating individuals around you.

Establish Achievable and Realistic objectives: Make sure your objectives are in line with your beliefs, interests, and strengths. Divide more ambitious objectives into more doable segments, and acknowledge and appreciate your accomplishments along the way.

Learn from Setbacks: See failures and setbacks as chances for development, learning, and introspection. Consider the lessons you can apply to future initiatives, pinpoint areas where you can grow, and consider the lessons you can gain from difficult situations.

Remain Perspective: Remain perspective-filled by acknowledging that failures and impediments are transitory and a necessary component of the process of developing resilience and progress. Remember the wider picture of your long-term objectives and desires while placing setbacks in perspective.

Exercise Self-Care: Make self-care and wellbeing a priority by doing things that feed your body, mind, and soul. Schedule time for the things that make you happy, content, and relaxed, such as hiking, gardening, or spending time with close friends and family.

Remain Adaptive and Flexible: Remain adaptable and flexible while handling obstacles and disappointments. Accept change, ambiguity, and unforeseen challenges as chances for both professional and personal development.

Honor Little wins: Honor accomplishments and wins of every size, regardless of how little they may seem. Recognize and value your advancement, fortitude, and resolve in overcoming setbacks and continuing on.

People with ADHD may develop optimism, overcome obstacles in life with bravery and grace, and develop inner strength by adopting a positive outlook and perseverance in the face of failures. Resilience is a skill that can be developed and reinforced over time with practice, introspection, and considerate self-care.

Looking towards the future with optimism and confidence in one's ability to thrive with ADHD

Looking towards the future with optimism and confidence in one's ability to thrive with ADHD is an empowering mindset that can lead to resilience, growth, and success. Here are some key strategies for embracing a positive outlook and building confidence in navigating life with ADHD:

Focus on Strengths: Recognize and celebrate your unique strengths and talents. Individuals with ADHD often possess qualities such as creativity, spontaneity, and resilience. Embrace these strengths and leverage them to overcome challenges and achieve your goals.

Cultivate Self-Awareness: Develop a deeper understanding of your strengths, weaknesses, and tendencies related to ADHD. Identify patterns, triggers, and strategies that work best for managing your symptoms and maximizing your potential.

Set Realistic Goals: Set realistic and achievable goals for yourself based on your interests, values, and aspirations. Break larger goals down into smaller, manageable steps, and celebrate each milestone along the way.

Practice Self-Compassion: Be kind and compassionate towards yourself, especially during times of struggle or setbacks. Understand that managing ADHD can be challenging, and it's okay to make mistakes or encounter obstacles along the way. Treat yourself with the same kindness and understanding that you would offer to a friend facing similar challenges.

Seek Support and Connection: Surround yourself with a supportive network of friends, family members, mentors, and professionals who understand and respect your journey with ADHD. Seek out support groups, online communities, and resources where you can connect with others who share similar experiences and challenges.

Focus on Solutions: Instead of dwelling on problems or setbacks, focus on finding solutions and implementing strategies to overcome obstacles. Maintain a proactive mindset and approach challenges as opportunities for growth and learning.

Celebrate Progress: Celebrate your progress and accomplishments, no matter how small they may seem. Recognize the efforts you've made and the steps you've taken towards managing ADHD and achieving your goals.

Stay Flexible and Adaptive: Be willing to adapt and adjust your strategies as needed based on changing circumstances or new information. Flexibility and adaptability are key traits that can help you navigate the ups and downs of life with ADHD.

Practice Mindfulness and Gratitude: Incorporate mindfulness practices and gratitude exercises into your daily routine to cultivate a sense of presence, acceptance, and appreciation for the present moment. Focus on the positives in your life and express gratitude for the blessings and opportunities that come your way.

Believe in Yourself: Above all, believe in yourself and your ability to thrive with ADHD. Trust in your resilience, resourcefulness, and capacity for growth. Approach each day with a sense of optimism, knowing that you have the strength and determination to overcome challenges and create a fulfilling life on your own terms.

By embracing a positive mindset and confidence in your ability to thrive with ADHD, you can cultivate resilience, foster personal growth, and unlock your full potential to live a meaningful and fulfilling life.

www.ingramcontent.com/pod-product-compliance
Lightning Source LLC
Chambersburg PA
CBHW050922260726
48660CB00001B/347